MEDITATIVE DRAWING
Guided Sketching to Calm the Busy Mind

Nam Doan

Copyright © 2017 by Nam Doan
All rights reserved. This book or any portion there of may
not be reproduced or used in any manner whatsoever
without the express written permission of the author.

Printed in the United States of America

First Printing, 2017

ISBN-13: 978-1546600251
ISBN-10: 1546600256

instagram.com/namroc

INTRODUCTION

By doing two simple things; drawing and breathing, this book can help you meditate almost anytime and anywhere.

For many years while I worked as an illustrator and animator, I began to notice there were times where I would enter into a state of bliss while I was drawing. The feeling was akin to being in a state of meditation. I felt calm, focused, present and at my most creative.

I found the technique in this book to be helpful prior to high-pressure situations such as a work presentation, crucial decision making or in times of anxiety and distress. It is especially helpful when used in situations otherwise difficult to create a traditional meditation space and you simply need a few minutes to calm your busy mind.

MEDITATIVE APPROACH

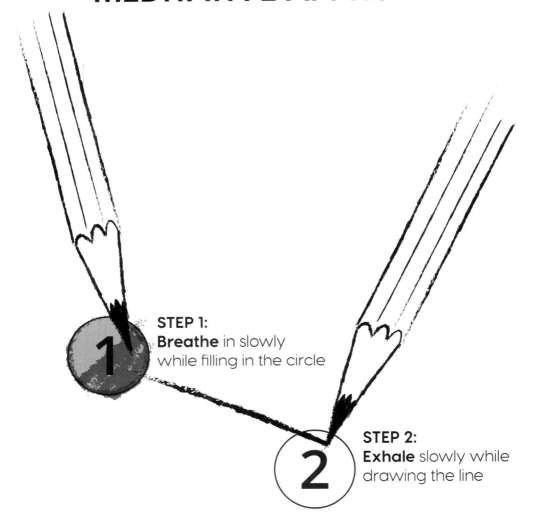

STEP 1:
Breathe in slowly while filling in the circle

STEP 2:
Exhale slowly while drawing the line

HELPFUL TIPS

- Take your time in performing the exercise
- Use a pencil in order to reuse the page
- Counting along with the exercise can help
- Start and stop whenever you like
- If the mind starts to wander, shift your thoughts back to your breathing and drawing

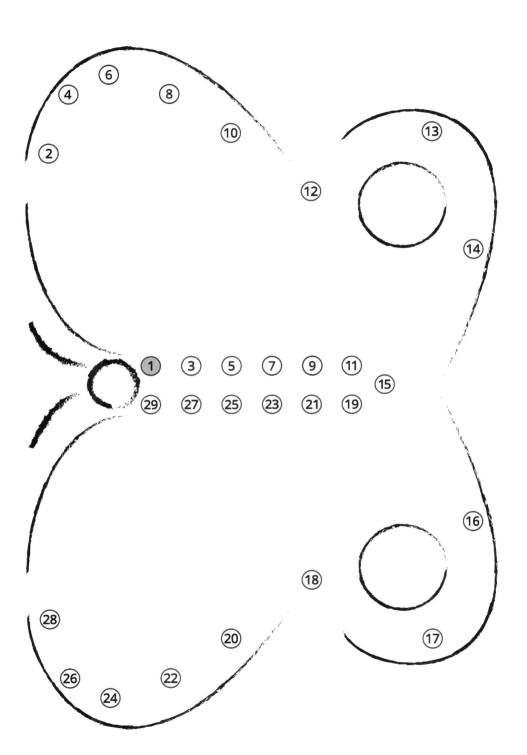

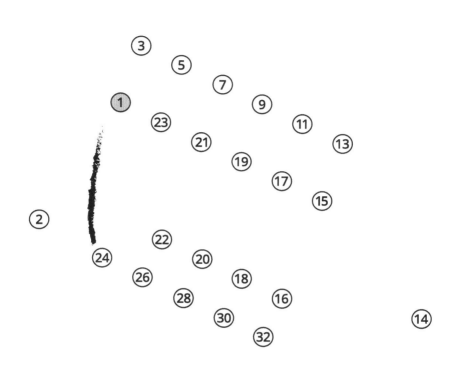

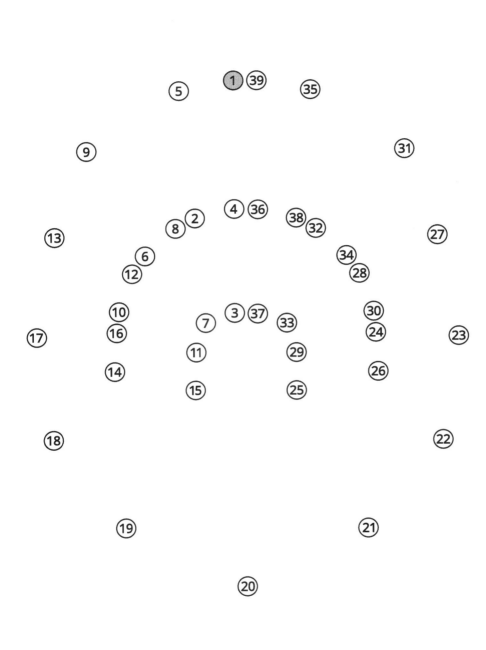

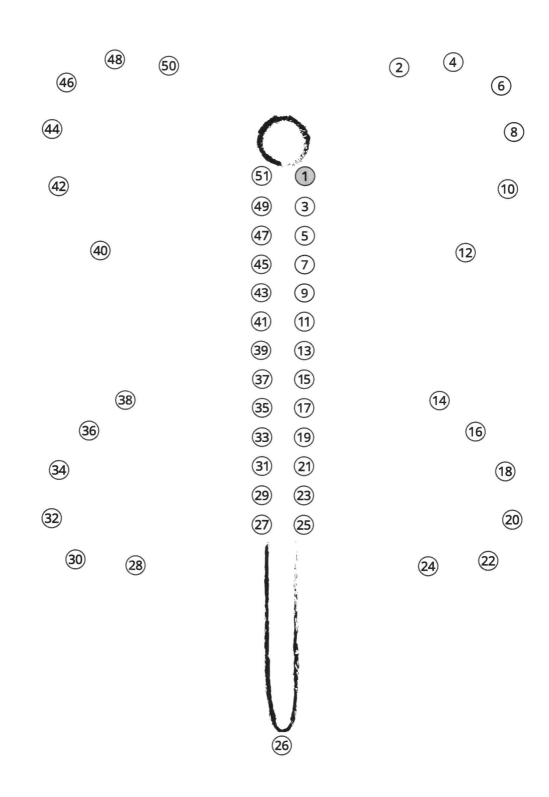

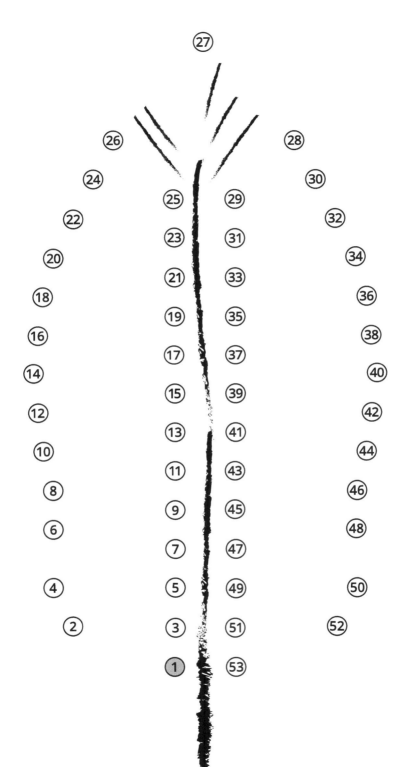

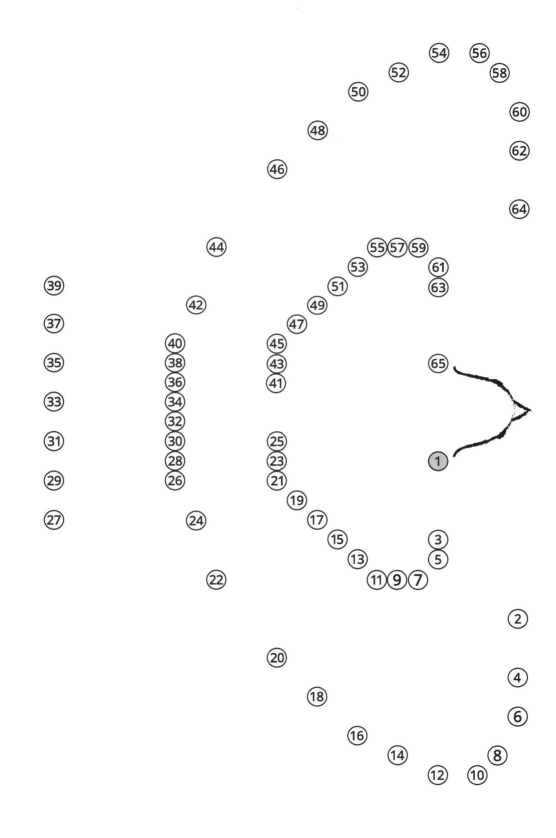

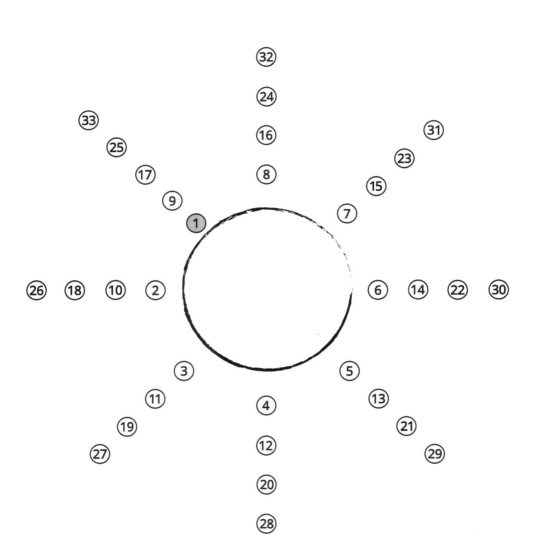

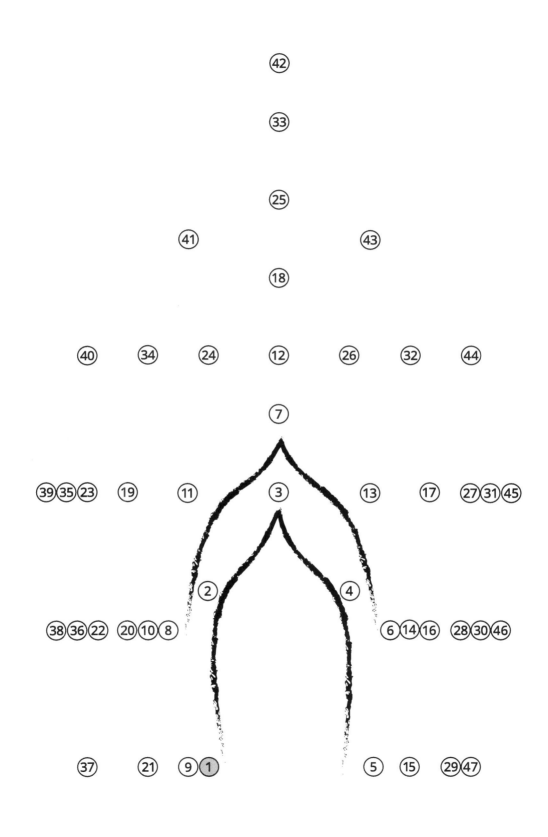

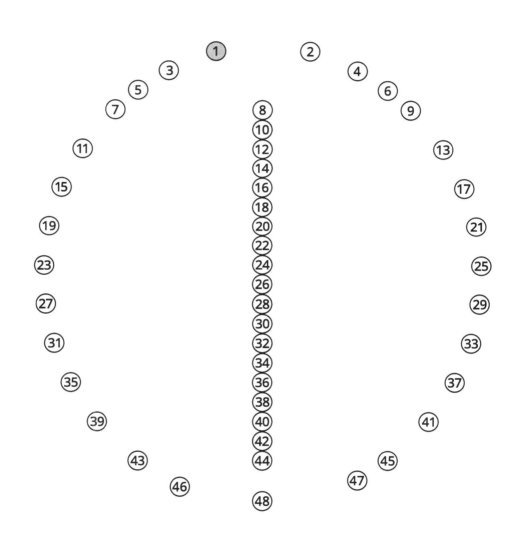

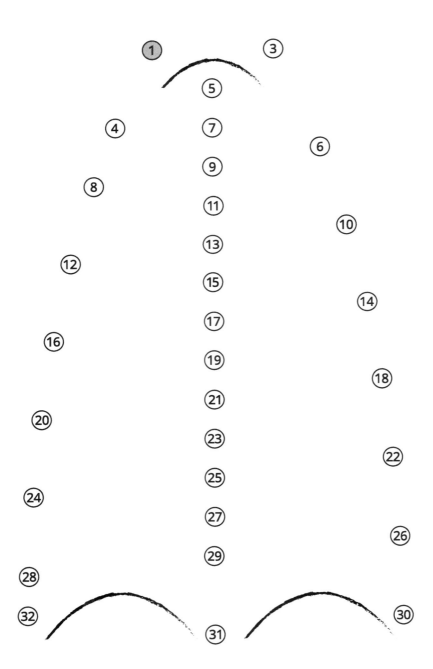

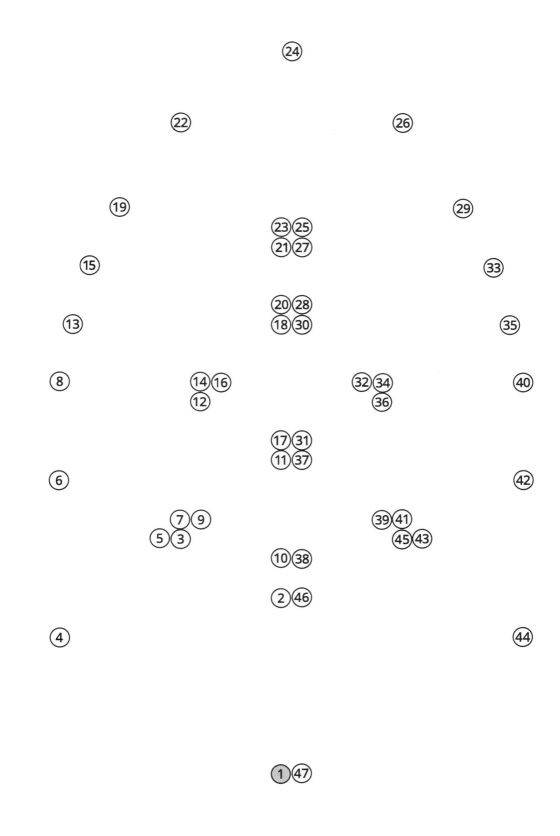

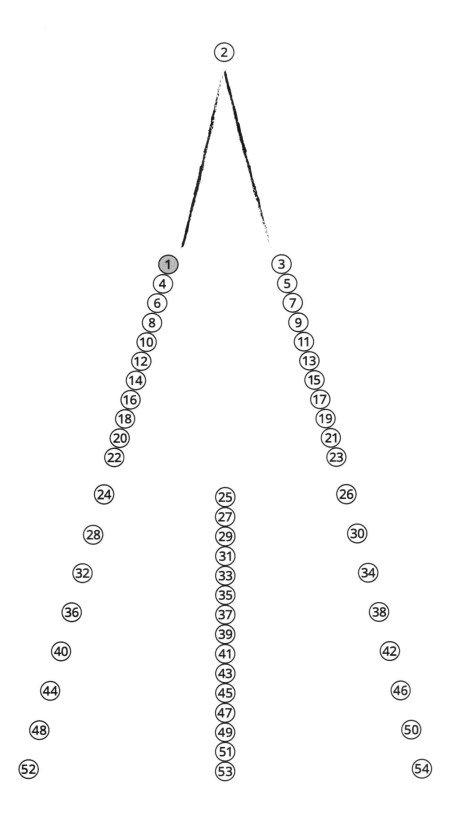

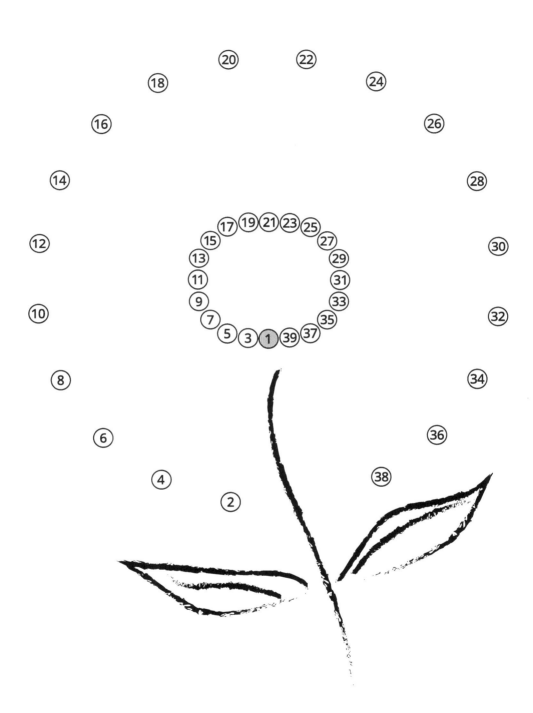

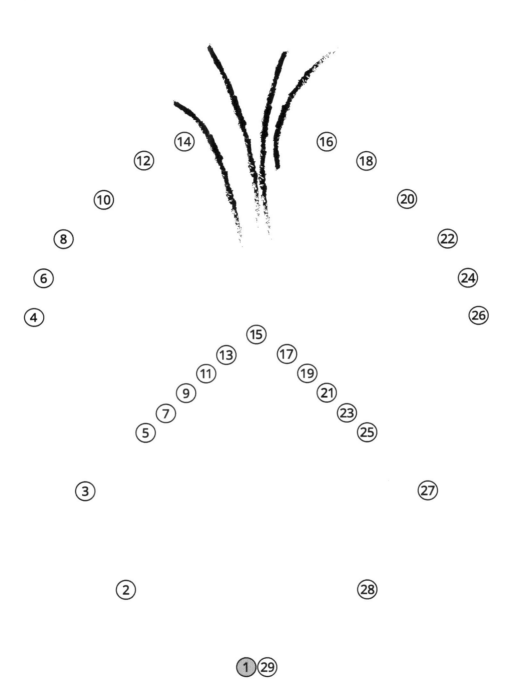

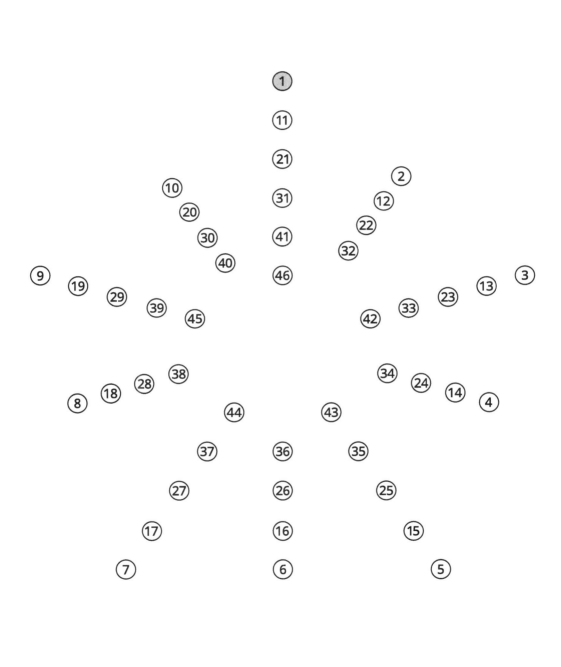

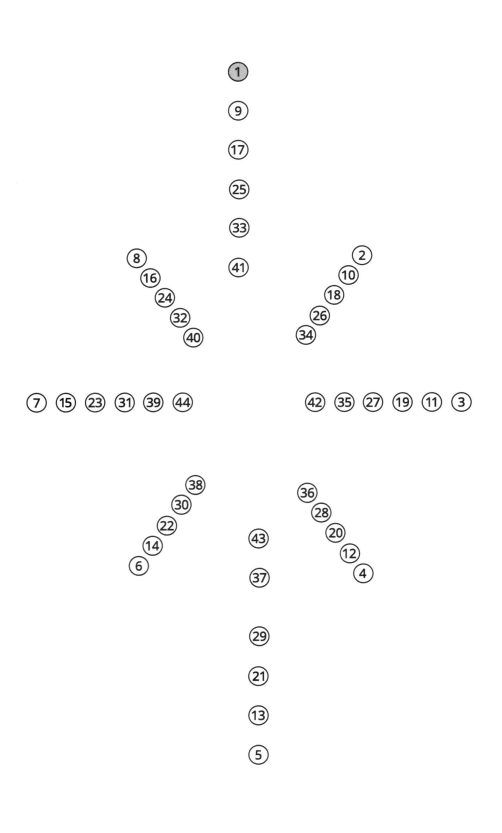

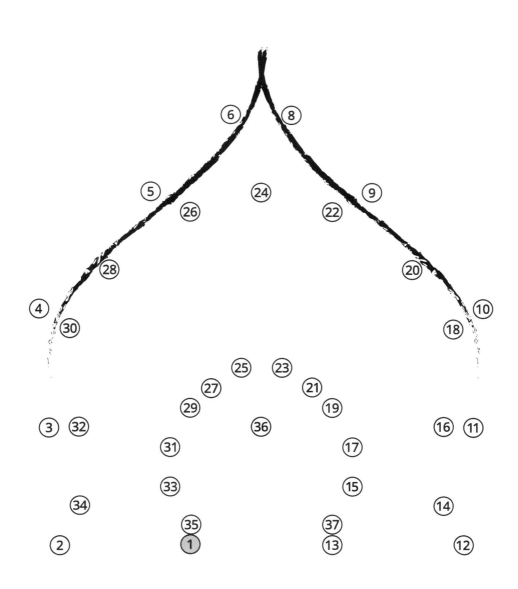

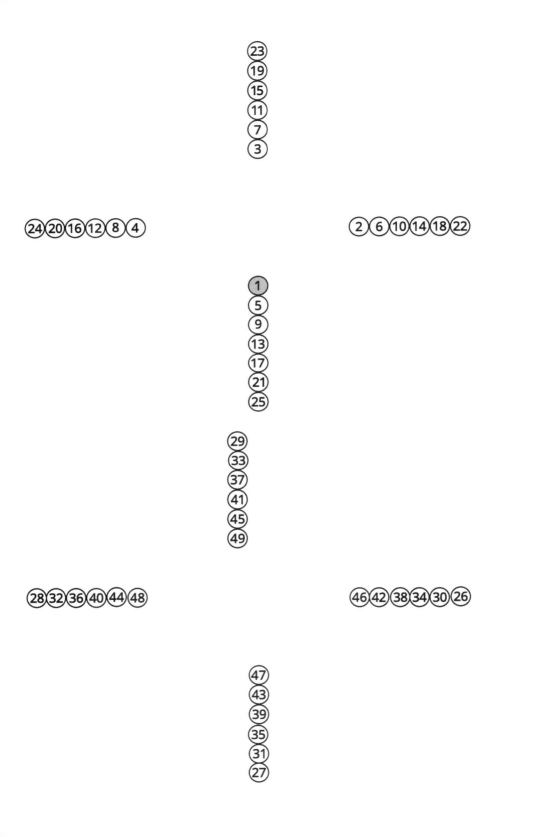

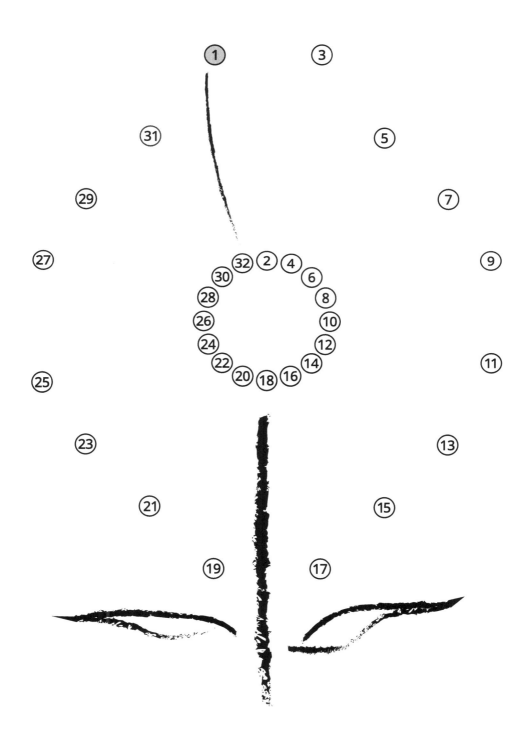

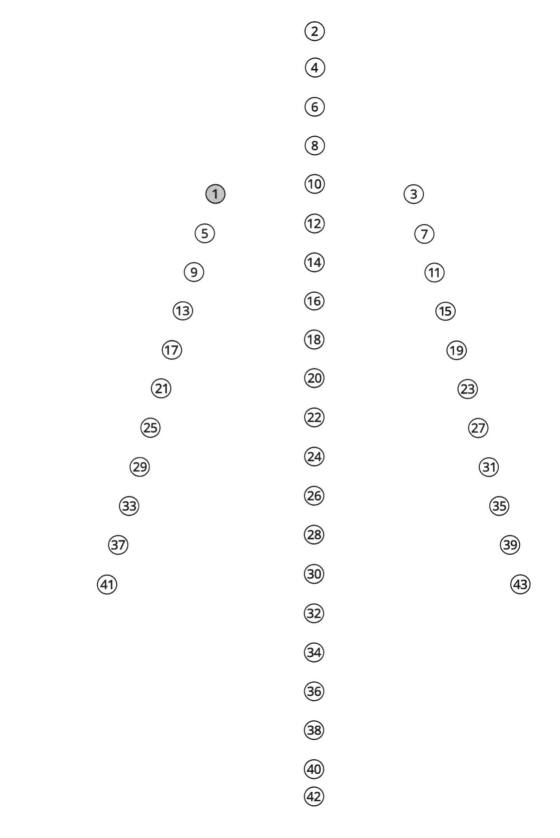

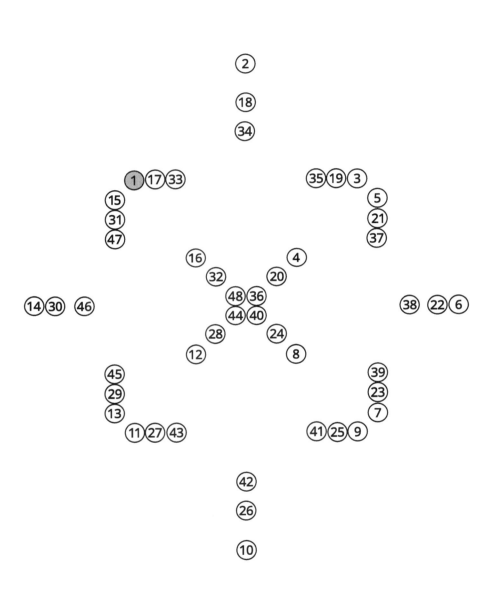

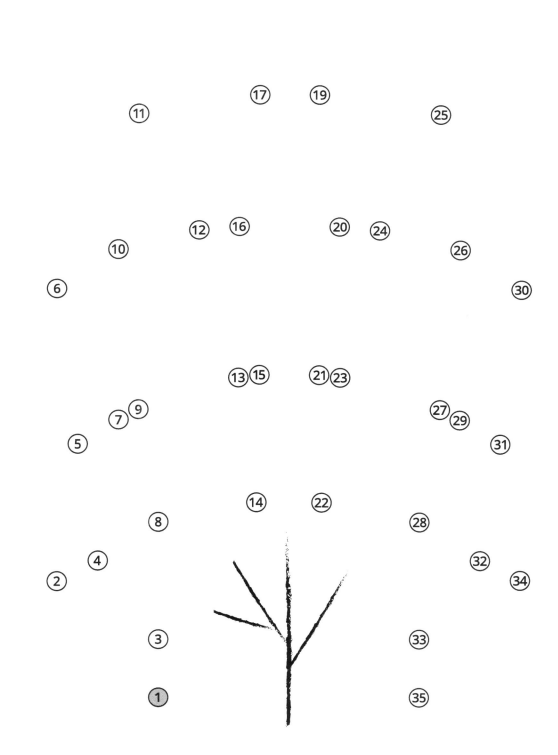

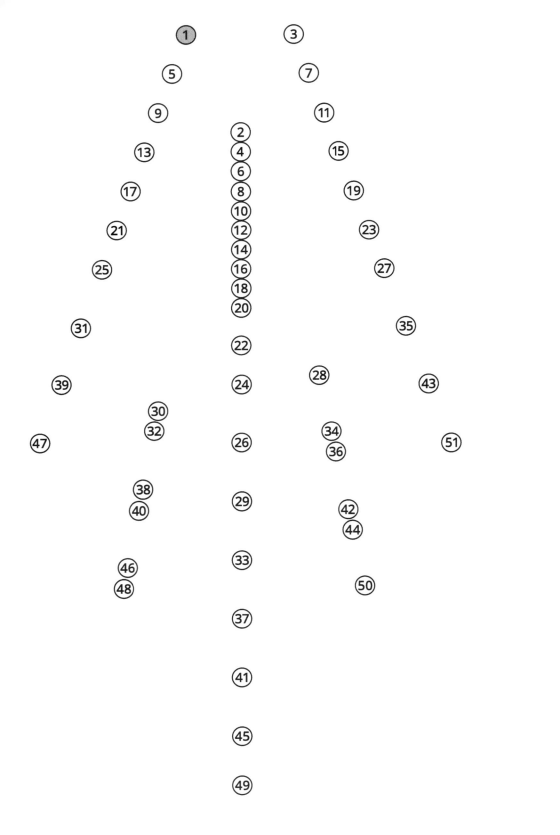

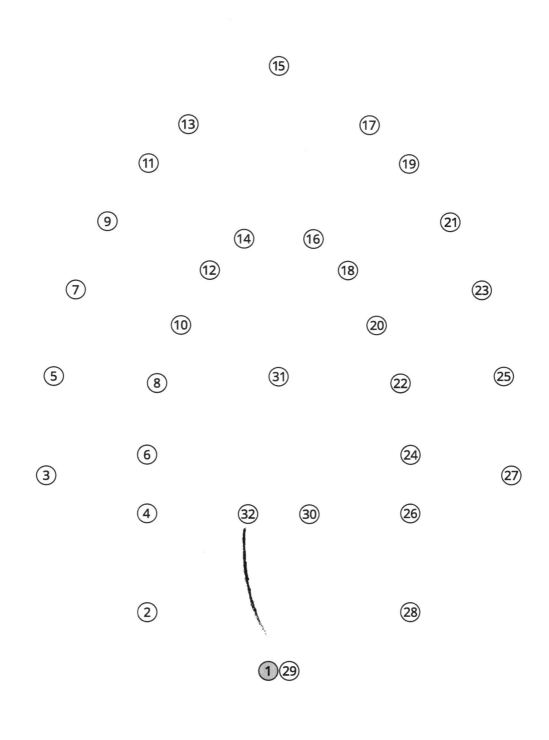

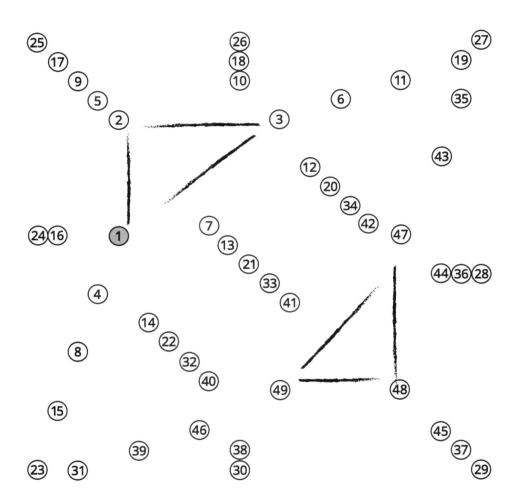

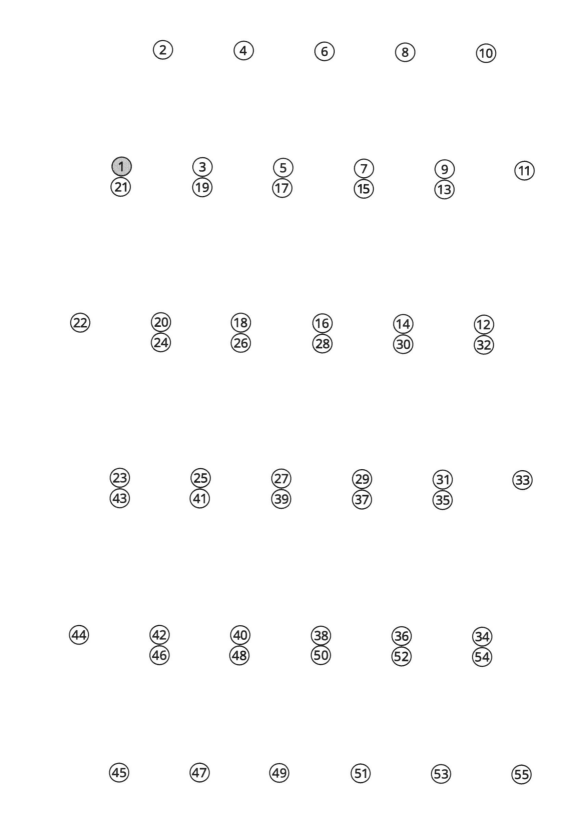

6

15

5 23 7

30

4 16 22   36   24 14 8

41

3 17 21 31 35   45   37 29 25 13 9

48

2 18 20 32 34 42 44   50   46 40 38 28 26 12 10

52

1 19   33 43 49   53   51 47   39   27   11

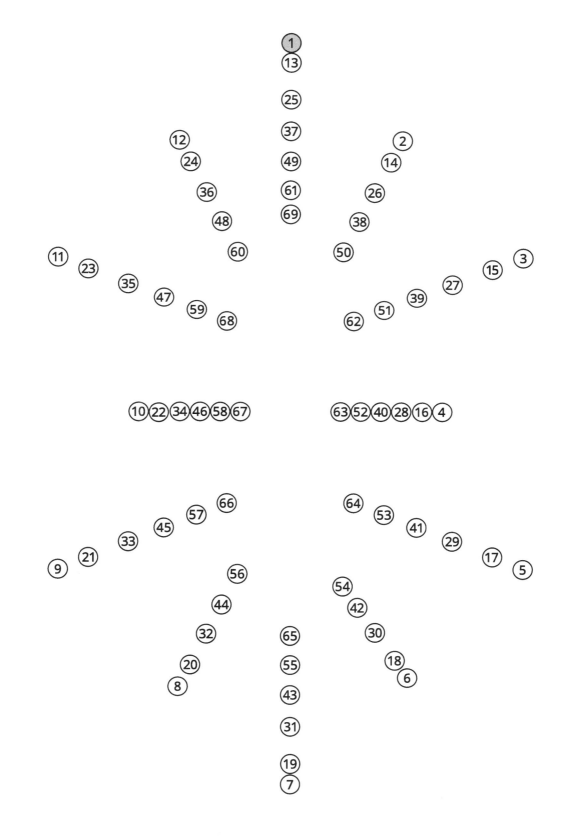

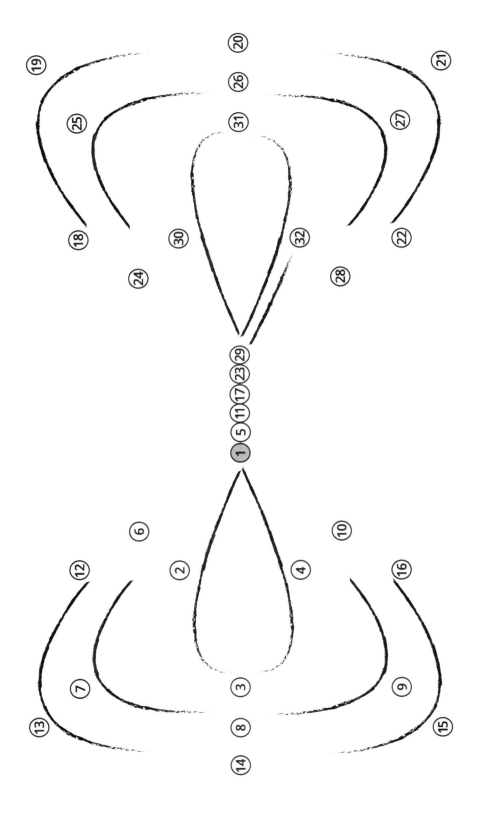

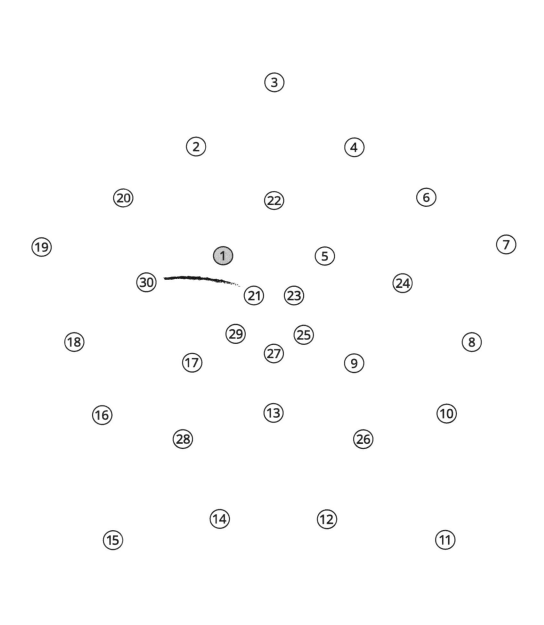

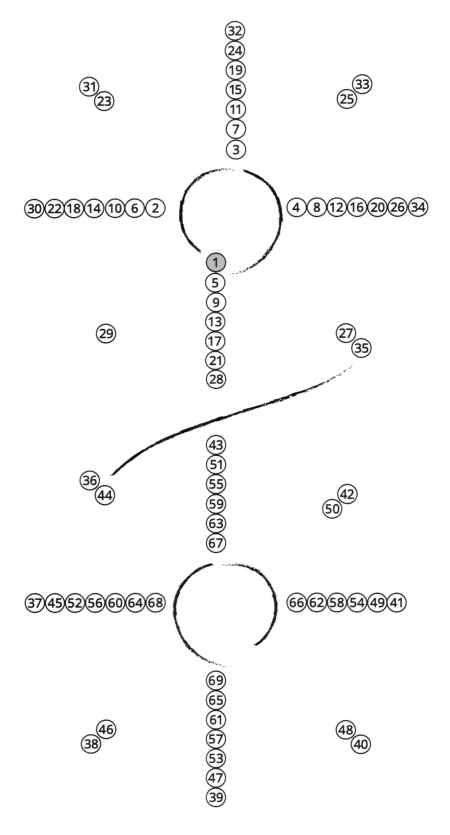

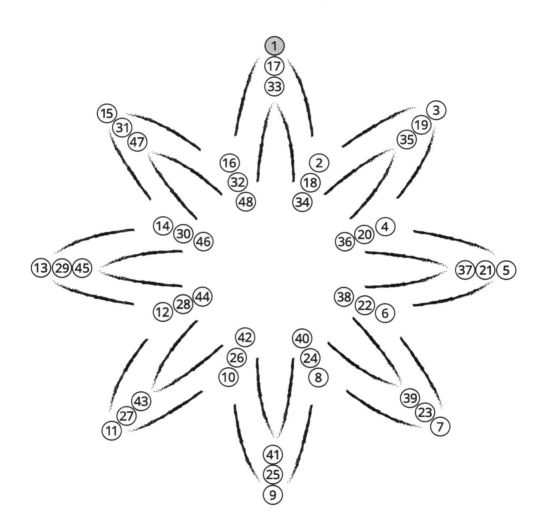

(11)　(27)　(39)(47)(51)　　　(49)(43)　(33)(19)(1)

(10)(12)(26)(28)(38)(40)(46)　(50)　　(44)(42)(34)(32)(20)(18)(2)

(48)

(9)(13)(25)(29)(37)　(45)　(35)(31)(21)(17)(3)

(41)

(8)(14)(24)　(36)　(22)(16)(4)

(30)

(7)　(23)　(5)

(15)

(6)

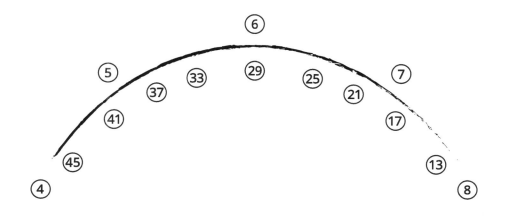
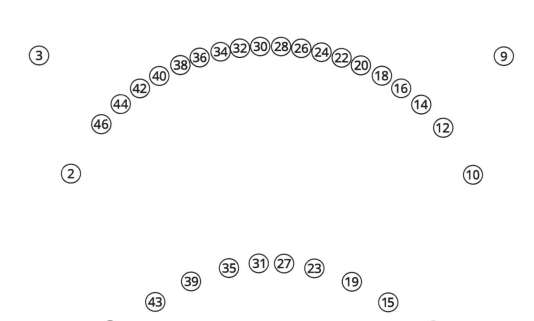

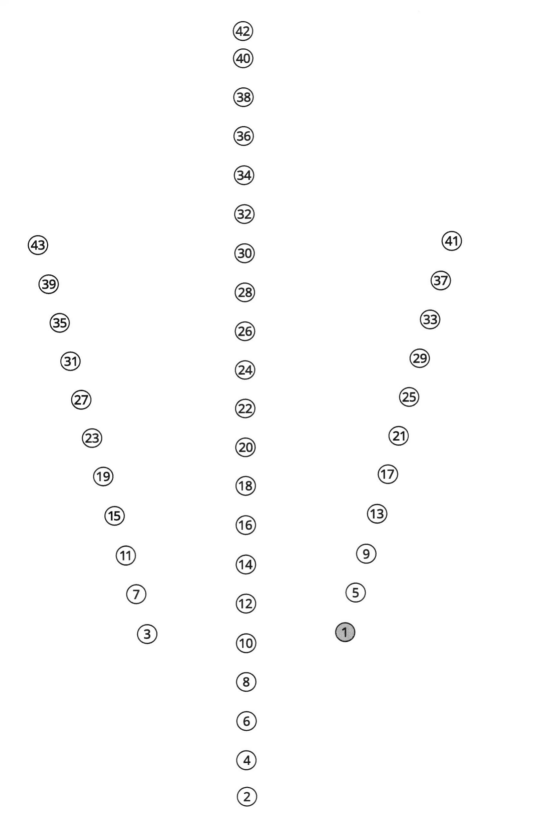

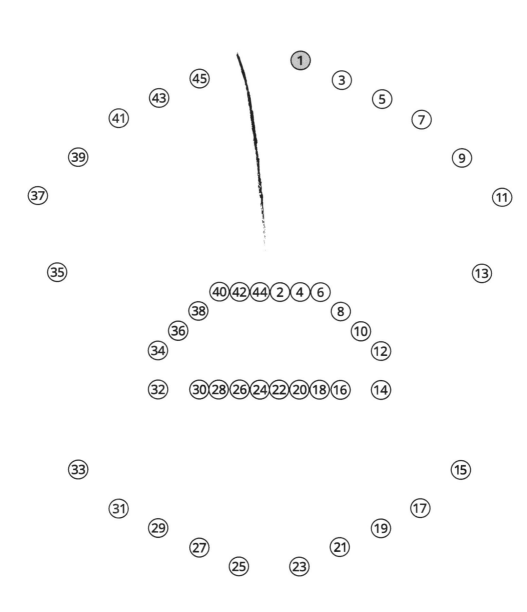

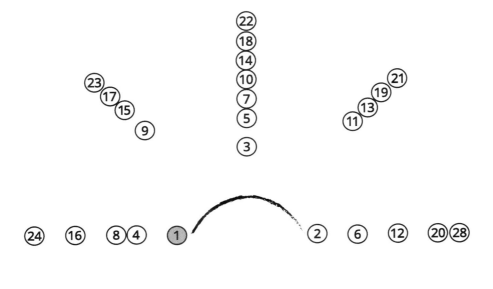

Printed in Great Britain
by Amazon